Celebrating Saints

Celebrating Saints

Thoughts and Prayers for Youth

Richard W. Bimler

Publishing House
St. Louis

Dedicated to two
of the many saints
who have helped the Bimlers
celebrate over the years—
Mrs. Mildred Bimler, my Mom
Mrs. Hazel Reichmann, my Mom-in-Law

Introduction

Recently I saw a poster that read, "If you love Jesus, why don't you tell your face about it?"

This does not mean that people of God continue walking around this world guffawing, laughing, shouting, and giggling 24 hours a day. It doesn't mean that we are oblivious to the pain and problems of today. It doesn't mean that we don't take anything very seriously.

But if there is anyone in this whole world who has something to celebrate, it's you and I and all of the people of God! For we have been redeemed, we are free, we are forgiven to live a life for others because our Lord has lived His life for us. His death and resurrection make it a fact—we are saved! And that is something to celebrate!

Christ's death and resurrection have moved us from being somber sinners to celebrating saints. We continue to be sinner and saint at the same time, but we are *forgiven* sinners, which makes us celebrating saints.

There are two kinds of people in this world: first, those who think they are saints and second, those who know they are sinners. Celebrating saints are sinners who know that they are sinners and that they have been forgiven in Jesus Christ.

The following pages are meant as celebrations for saints. The thoughts and prayers shared here hopefully can encourage and push each of us to celebrate our relationship with Jesus Christ with others.

You are a saint. It is a name God gives to you. This may not be a popular name with peers who may sneer and mistake you for a "holier-than-thou" type with your halo showing. Who wants to be called a "saint" or to be known as one? Especially a young person! Especially when the idea is prevalent that saints are "sticks-in-the-mud" and that surely they do not have much fun.

So why would anyone want to read this book? In short, the word "saint" is not attractive to most people and it suffers from caricatures and stereotypes. And for others, "celebrations" may apply more to rock concerts than to a Christian life-style for young people today.

This book is dedicated to the belief that God's people, saints, need to help persons see and sense the real purpose and definition of a "saint." A person is a saint because of Christ's death and resurrection. A saint is not only someone who has died, or some-one who appears in a stained-glass window in a church building. A saint is a "real" person, made alive and forgiven by Jesus Christ.

1 Peter 2:9–10 says it so well: "You are a chosen race, a royal priesthood, a holy nation, God's own people, that you may declare the wonderful deeds of Him who called you out of darkness into His marvelous light. Once you were no people but now you are God's people; once you had not received mercy but now you have received mercy."

Celebrations for celebrating saints are not always raucous, loud, and boisterous events. I don't always feel like shouting "Praise the Lord" or "Hallelujah." Sometimes my celebration comes in a quiet whisper, a soft word, a loving look. Celebrating saints are people who know that the Lord is present with us, even when we don't feel like it or act like it or look like it.

It is hoped that the following pages will help the reader celebrate sainthood. This book is intentionally not geared only to young people or to adults, because youth and adults need each other to celebrate the joys and power and presence of our Lord—a Lord who allows both youth and adults to celebrate together.

So celebrate as you read and read as you celebrate. Share this good news with other youth and adults around you.

Outline of the Book

A few years ago a paperback book hit the market and was an instant success. It was entitled *Real Men Don't Eat Quiche*. A few years later, another best seller appeared, this one aptly titled *Real Women Don't Pump Gas*. Even before these books appeared—and certainly after they had appeared—many conversations and discussions continued to center around the question, "What characteristics really do make people *real?*" What are the behaviors of the "typical" young person? How should "good" parents react? What characteristics do we look for as we decide what "real people" really are?

The following pages pick up on this theme and respond to the open-ended sentence: "Real saints . . . ." There are specific characteristics and traits that celebrating saints have, and these can be shared with those who are not celebrating around us. These pages affirm and reaffirm that only God in Jesus Christ makes us "saints." It is His life, suffering, death, and resurrection that have sealed our "saintness." Therefore, these pages celebrate the fact that none of our gifts, traits, or characteristics makes us saints: instead, God's forgiveness and love in Christ have done it all for us.

A Prayer to End This Section

Sure Lord, it's easy to say, "Celebrate." But it's really hard to live it out in our lives. Maybe it's easy for people to say it when things are going well. But how do I celebrate when everything is falling in around me? Help me, Lord, not to see "Celebrate" as another commandment from You. But rather help me see that celebration can come only from Your love and forgiveness. Don't let people tell me to celebrate or coerce me into it. Instead, help them show through their lives that their celebration is grounded in your death and resurrection.

Maybe then, Lord, and only then, can I see celebration as more than a word, as more than a command.

Help me celebrate, Lord, now! Amen.

Contents

Part 1

Chapter 1

Celebrating Saints Rejoice in Their Lord

Celebration starts with knowing who we are. Throughout the Scriptures the Lord continues to affirm that we are His people and that He is our God. Listen to Colossians 3:12 for example: "[You are] God's chosen ones, holy and beloved ..." Did you hear that? We are His people—right now, today! These words from the Lord are not commands or threats, but rather words of affirmation. He, and only He, has made us His people. Notice it does not say that we "need to try a little harder" and then we will be the people of God, or "we better shape up" and then we will be the people of God. No! God has done it for us. We are His people now, today, forever because of what Christ Jesus has done for us. Christ came to live, suffer, die, and rise so that we now are His people.

Look a little further in Colossians 3. St. Paul, right after affirming and reminding us who we are, begins to list many characteristics of people of God. In verses 12-15 he lists many exciting characteristics such as compassion, kindness, humility, gentleness, patience, thankfulness, peace, and on and on and on.

It is important to note that God does not say that as soon as we begin showing some of these traits we will be assured that we are

God's people; rather, God announces to us that *because* we are His people in Christ we are able, by the power of Holy Spirit, to share these great gifts with others.

I had always read these verses as kind of a checklist of how I was doing each day. B in compassion, C- in kindness, a failing grade in humility, and an incomplete on patience. But this is not a scorecard for us, but rather a list of gifts that are ours because we *are* the people of God.

It's also helpful to note that our being His people has nothing to do with what we have done or will ever do. Even when we don't act like, feel like, or look like God's people, we are still His people. For our faith is not dependent on how we look or act or feel, but on the fact of Christ's death and resurrection for us.

This is where our celebration and joy comes from. To be a celebrating saint means to be forgiven. It means that we are forgiven even when we don't look like a celebrating saint or act like a celebrating saint or even feel like a celebrating saint.

I have never yet been in a worship service where we have sung, "I Wish That My Redeemer Lives" or "It Sure Would Be Nice If My Redeemer Lived." No, we continually affirm and shout out the fact that "I Know That My Redeemer Lives!" It is this fact that is the source of our celebrating.

Celebrating saints are Resurrection Resources. Christ's resurrection becomes our resurrection. His death has wiped out our fear of our own death. Because He lives we too live, as celebrating saints and Resurrection Resources.

A Prayer

Lord, thanks for calling me as one of Your people. It's good to know that I do not need to be a certain age or act in a certain way or look a certain way or even feel a certain way in order for You to love me.

Because You love me, I am now able to reach out to others with compassion, kindness, love, patience and forgiveness. Even when I fail in sharing these, the fact that You continue to call me as one of Your own is the power I need to continue to live in forgiveness and in celebration.

I am a Resurrection Resource. I am one of Your people. And I'm glad! Amen.

Chapter 2

Celebrating Saints Celebrate Life Now

Someone once said, "I am not looking forward to eternal life, I'm enjoying it right now!" These are helpful words for us celebrating saints. We are celebrating eternal life right now because our Lord is with us. This does not take away from that glorious time when we will be reunited in heaven with our Lord. But we can celebrate our relationship with the Lord right now and not have to wait until we die.

Many people around us, both youth and adults, do not have a sense of celebration each day. Some have gotten themselves into ruts, some are bored with life, some have been stomped on for so long that they are tired of fighting. Some older persons who have retired and feel that they have been "shelved" by their family, church, and community, also struggle with sensing that the Lord has given them the power to celebrate.

Young people too find themselves bored and struggling. One stereotype of young people has them all full of pep, excited, happy, joyful, without a care in the world. That is the furthest thing from the truth for many young people. For they too, because of their sins, are struggling with the problems, the pains, the frustrations of

17

life. God's word to them is more than a trite, "Celebrate son, things will get better." What these people need around them more are celebrative people of God-who can quietly care for, listen to, and be aware of these kinds of persons and reach out with a quiet love and understanding.

As part of the Kennedy evangelism program, a usual question asked is, "If you were to die tonight, would you go to heaven?" This is an excellent question. But another pointed question to ask people is: "If you are alive tomorrow, how do you plan to celebrate that gift?"

For celebrating saints continue to celebrate in spite of sins and death around them. They celebrate because they see life as a gift from God. They celebrate because they have been redeemed through the death and resurrection of Jesus Christ. They celebrate, not to ignore the pain and the Good Fridays of their lives, but rather to rejoice in the victory which the resurrection of Christ has given them over the pain and the deaths and the Good Fridays in their lives!

After every Good Friday, there is an Easter. And that's the truth!

A Prayer

Lord, help me to celebrate life now. Help me to see life as a gift to be used, to be shared, to be enjoyed. Help me to help others do the same thing for their own lives. Perhaps my celebration today will not be with balloons and banners and confetti; rather, allow me to celebrate by sharing a quiet word with a distraught friend, a soft hug with a family member, a caring glance with a new companion.

Perhaps tomorrow, Lord, You will allow me to celebrate in other ways. By blowing up a balloon, by flying a kite, by kissing a baby, by shouting hooray.

Let me be ready to celebrate Your way. Let me be ready to celebrate my faith to people so that they do not get caught up in the way I celebrate, but in whom I am celebrating. Amen.

Chapter 3

Celebrating Saints Celebrate Both Death and Resurrection

Let's take a little journey of faith. Let's walk the path of Jesus from His death on the cross to His powerful resurrection. Put on your walking shoes and follow me; we've got quite a journey ahead of us. But it is a journey that again shows the reasons why we continue to celebrate as God's special, redeemed people. Let's start walking . . .

Step 1—Jesus Is Condemned

It's hard to imagine an innocent person being falsely accused and condemned to death and to think that they let a killer go free so they could crucify our Lord. But Barabbas was set free, and Christ was condemned to death.

The authorities of that day said, "Christ deserved to die." But by His death we have life.

This fact from the past is more than a history lesson. It's more than a TV superseries spectacular. Christ's condemnation was God at work freeing us from our chains of sin.

But look around us. Maybe Barabbas is free. But how often do you and I continue to live our lives as if we were still chained in the power of sin and death? How often do we live chained to our own selfish ways?

We once had a dog named Spud. Spud lived outside all of his life and was quite old. One day his chain broke. But guess what? He continued to run around that worn dirt path as he had always done, not realizing that his chain was broken, and that he was free. How often do we do the same thing?

Two caterpillars were talking one day. One looked up and saw a butterfly, flying freely and graciously above them. The one caterpillar turned to the other one and said, "You'll never get me up in one of those things."

Watch out, caterpillars. Watch out, Spud the dog. Watch out, Barabbas. Watch out, all of us. Don't be too surprised what happens. Christ's death has made us free—free indeed!

Step 2—Jesus Takes Up His Cross

Did you "give up" something for Lent this year? This certainly can be a fine custom to remind us of Christ giving up His life for us. But let's consider something else. Instead of giving something up, let's "take up" something. Let's take up Christ's cross, as He took up the cross for us. Let's take up His cross, through the power of the Spirit, and move that cross in and through our daily lives. How do we do this? First, by "giving up" ourselves. Yes, that's right. We take up the cross by giving up ourselves. Our prayer is, "Lord, I give up! I can do nothing without you. My sin crushes me. My sin is hurting me and others. I give up!"

This cry of surrender is heard by our Lord, who took up our crosses and made them His own. We give up, and then our Lord enables us to take up the cross for others.

What are the crosses in your life? Is it physical pain, emotional stress, suffering because you love the Lord, loneliness, or friction in the family? Christ is picking up those crosses for you. Do you see all the crosses in our world, such as hunger, pain, hatred, grief, fear, sorrow? Christ allows us to pick up those crosses for others too. For people who sometimes feel like jumping off the edge of the world,

Christ comes and announces that He has smoothed out all the edges.

"Give up," the Lord says to us right now, "because I have taken up your cross. Now get up and pick up the crosses of others."

Step 3—Carrying the Cross

Christ was being led out to die, and no one had come to walk with Him. From Bethlehem, where angels had rejoiced at his birth, no one came. From Nazareth, where He had lived, no one came. From Cana of Galilee, where He performed His first miracle, no one came. In all the world there was no one to walk with Him along the road to the cross.

But wait! There was one. There he is now! Here came a man who had never seen Jesus before. He had never heard a parable, he had never seen a miracle. This one man was to walk where no other human being dared to walk. He was to walk the road of the cross.

Up from Joppa came Simon, from the sunlit shores of northern Africa, to visit the Holy City at the time of the Passover. He was probably on a vacation. Just as he entered the city, he was rudely halted by a strange procession. As he stood watching, he was suddenly seized by Roman soldiers. Did he protest? Of course he did, but it did him no good. The soldiers told him roughly that the business at hand had to be hurried along and that he must carry a cross. They placed it on his shoulders, and instead of enjoying the pleasures of a holiday, Simon suddenly found that he was walking a way he did not want to go. Before him went the bowed and thorn-crowned figure of a stranger. It was a real cross that Simon was carrying. It was not a pretty, golden one worn by people today; not the great ornamental crosses raised in adoration on the high towers of our churches. Simon was walking the way of the cross. It was a cross of coarse, hard, and heavy timber. As he walked, the shouts of the yelling people were no more bitter than the thoughts of Simon's heart. He had planned a holiday, and here he was carrying a cross for a condemned criminal.

But slowly his thoughts changed. The cross was pressing on his neck. He could not turn his head to the right or to the left. He could only look straight ahead. Before him was no one but that silent figure in the purple robe and the crown of thorns. It was his great God-given moment along with Christ. The hands of the living God had carried him here to Jerusalem for a single purpose: to stand and walk with Jesus for a moment, to look upon the tear-stained face of the unwanted, lonely sin-bearer. To look and to be saved. The way of the cross had made him a disciple. The everlasting and gracious purposes of God had been accomplished again.

We too are asked to carry the cross of Christ. The road is rough, the path is rugged. But we go, knowing that the Lord has already passed this way for us.

Step 4—Jesus Meets the Women of Jerusalem

After every Good Friday, there is an Easter. We know this as a fact because we live on this side of Christ's death and resurrection. But it was different for the people in Jesus' time. They did not know yet that His death was one that led to an Easter resurrection. As we mourn Christ's death and repent of our sins that sent Him to die, we also need to see that Christ turns our mourning into joy. Mourning has broken! Indeed it has, and we will gloriously celebrate that fact every Easter Sunday. And, for that matter, we celebrate it every Sunday as we worship together.

Jeremiah reminds us that mourning for people of God turns to joy. This is not because of what we have done but because of what Christ has done for us. "I will turn their mourning into joy, I will comfort them, and give them gladness for sorrow" (Jer. 31:13b).

So our fasting during Lent turns into a feast of Easter. Because of Christ we can now

fast from criticism, feast on praise;
fast from self-pity, feast on joy;
fast from ill temper, feast on peace;
fast from resentment, feast on contentment;
fast from jealousy, feast on love;
fast from pride, feast on humility;
fast from selfishness, feast on service;
fast from fear, feast on faith;
fast from death, feast on resurrection!

Yes, those who sow in tears shall reap with shouts of joy. Listen for the whisper, the quiet comfort of joy that comes through to us after every Good Friday in our lives.

Step 5—Jesus Is Nailed to the Cross

"Forgive them; for they know not what they do" (Luke 23:34). Can you imagine this? Here our Lord is nearing death and He is still thinking of others. He reaches out and asks the Heavenly Father to forgive those two criminals who are dying with Him. Our Lord is being nailed to the cross, and He continues to minister to those around Him.

In Jesus we see what God intended human beings to be: forgiving, loving, servants to others.

Forgiveness is the key to the Christian life. Forgiving is for living. The gift of the Spirit for each of us is forgiveness.

Our guilt has been taken away in forgiveness through Jesus Christ. Are we guilty? Yes, we certainly are. Our sin convicts us. We are sinful, undeserving beings. But are we guilty? "No!" says Christ, "for I have forgiven you through My death and resurrection."

Are we innocent? No. Our sins convict us. But yes, we are innocent, because Christ has shed His blood to take away our sins.

Guilty, yes, but no. Innocent, no, but yes. Forgiven—yes, yes, yes. All in the name of Jesus!

Step 6—Jesus Speaks from the Cross

We've heard again our Lord from the cross. There He is. Ready to die for us. As you hear Him speaking to you from that cross, what do you want to say to Him? What words or thoughts or visions do you want to share with Him right now? He is our Lord, who has died for us to free us for eternal life.

Take a few moments right now silently to speak to Your Lord on the cross. What do you want to ask Him, or say to Him? Now is your time to speak. Pause for a moment on your journey of life to talk silently with your Lord.

Step 7—Jesus Dies on the Cross

It is finished. Our Lord has died. He did it all for you and for me.

Why do we insist on calling that Friday "Good Friday?" What's so good about it? Why can't we call it "Bad Friday?" It's the day when all of our sins snuffed out Christ's life. Christ died because of Peter and Joseph and Simon and Paul and Ruth and Naomi and you and me. And we call this "good"?

Christ's words, "It is finished," also announce to us that now everything has been completed for our salvation. "It is finished" means that there is nothing we can do or need to do on our own. He has done it all. We are redeemed. The task is accomplished. It is finished!

And so "bad" Friday begins to be seen as "good" Friday. Notice all the little plants that sprout each spring after winter? Here we thought creation had died, but the first days of spring bring out the little plants and flowers that announce to us "new life." Life comes out of death. Sure, death is real; but so is life in the Lord Jesus!

Thus, after every Good Friday we wait to see what happens. God is even more powerful than our own sin.

What a difference a day makes—let alone three. Christ turns all bad Fridays into good ones. Just wait a few days and see.

The story goes that some people asked Jesus, "Are we condemned to go to hell?" And Jesus answered, "Over my dead body."

"The light shines in the darkness, and the darkness has not overcome it" (John 1:5).

Celebrating saints celebrate Good Friday in order that they can celebrate the Easter resurrection. Celebrating saints see that every bad Friday (or bad Monday, Tuesday, Wednesday, Thursday, Saturday or Sunday) is always turned into joy and resurrection, through the power of the Holy Spirit working through us.

Continue to walk the way of Good Friday in your daily lives. We can do so because the Lord always allows us to end up at the empty tomb, where we continue to celebrate the presence and power of His love and forgiveness.

A Prayer

Lord, keep us on your path. Help us to accept both the pains and the joys of life, the deaths and the resurrections, the nos and the yeses.

Keep us on the path, Lord, your path — to real life — to resurrected life. Amen.

Chapter 4 

Celebrating Saints Live from the Steeple to the People

A pastor was showing a visitor his church building. The visitor asked, "How many people does your church seat?" The pastor responded, "900 people. But the question I would rather answer is, 'How many people does our church send?'"

Celebrating saints are in the people-sending business. We gather on Sunday morning around Word and Sacrament to praise our God, to celebrate who we are as God's people, to be strengthened in our faith. We gather around the steeple, not as an end in itself, but rather as a means to an end. It is a means to minister to people. We gather in order to scatter.

Some youth and adults see Sunday morning worship as an end result. "I sure feel better when I worship on Sunday," is sometimes heard. "It just doesn't seem like Sunday if I don't go to church." These both are well-intentioned comments; yet celebrating saints sense that they need to gather around the steeple, the cross, and the empty tomb, in order to be strengthened and empowered for the ministry that is theirs. That ministry is to share and help others join in the celebration.

Imagine this. You are watching a football game. The offensive players get into their huddle. Fifteen seconds go by, 30 seconds go by, 60 seconds go by, five minutes go by, and these guys are still in the huddle.

You would begin to wonder, "What's going on?" They seem really to be enjoying themselves, patting each other on the back, and laughing and celebrating together. But that's not the purpose of a huddle. The purpose of a huddle is to plan your strategy and then work the plan. The huddle is a means to an end. The huddle is a place to gather so that you can play the game.

The church is a "holy huddle." We huddle together on Sunday morning, we huddle around the steeple of the Lord, but not just to enjoy ourselves and keep the "play" to ourselves. We gather in a holy huddle in order to move out to the people. It is just as ridiculous as a group of football players staying in the huddle as it is to think of a group of celebrating saints gathering on Sunday morning and then not sharing what they do during the rest of the week.

A holy huddle—that's what we are all about!

A Prayer

Lord, thanks for calling us to be a part of Your Holy Huddle. We need that. We need the comfort and the strengthening that a holy huddle offers. We need to share, to be built up, to be centered around the steeple.

But Lord, also send us out to the people. Help us to see that the holy huddle is one way to celebrate. The other way of celebrating is to share the good news of love and forgiveness with those around our lives. A holy huddle is comforting. A holy huddle is exciting. So also are the tasks before us. Thanks for calling us into Your huddle. Thanks for giving us the game plan. And thanks for sending us out, from the steeple to the people.

In Jesus' holy name. Amen.

Chapter 5

Celebrating Saints Keep a Positive Perspective on Life

It's easy to get our lives out of focus. It's easy to concentrate on minor things in our lives and ignore some of the major priorities and directions. I sometimes think that parents cause some anxious moments by overreacting to minor concerns while ignoring some of the major relationships among their own young people.

For example, a recent study indicated that young people wanted their parents to talk more about three subjects and issues. First, they wanted their parents to share their faith more. That's right. They were saying that their parents did not connect their faith and life together enough and that young people were hoping that their parents could discuss faith issues with them to a greater degree.

Second, young people wanted their parents to deal with sexuality issues. Once again they said that their parents were not assertive enough in sharing and talking about sexuality issues, including physical changes, emotional changes, dating, and how best to deal with other pressures in life.

Third, young people said that they wish their parents would talk more with them about vocations. They indicated that very few

27

adults are helping them in sorting out an occupation. Often high school counselors are too busy, churches aren't involved, and parents aren't talking. These young people were encouraging their parents to help them sort through their own gifts and plans for their future.

How does one keep a positive perspective on life? How can people of God continue to celebrate when the pains and strains of daily life are all so evident? How can we even talk about celebrating when thousands in the world are dying from hunger? How can one even dare to suggest that we have something to celebrate when so many families are being destroyed, so many people are being neglected, and so many people are being abused?

The word from the Lord comes to comfort us even in the midst of pain and agony. It's amazing, for example, how the psalmists pick up the many feelings of all of us. Throughout the psalms we hear cries of anger, of guilt, of pain, but also cries of joy and of thanksgiving. What makes the difference?

Our Lord continues to keep our lives in perspective. He continues to allow us to look at all of life through the cross and the empty tomb. He allows us to get off base and then He continues to woo us back with His love and forgiveness. It's the same way in the Scriptures. God's people blunder and mess things up and God continues to come back to them with His love and forgiveness.

A college student captured this whole area of keeping life in perspective by writing the following letter home.

Dear Mom and Dad,

Sorry it's been so long since I've written. The skull fracture and broken leg I got after I jumped out the window of my dormitory when it caught fire have almost healed. I was in the hospital only three weeks. I can see almost normally again, and those sick headaches come only once in a while.

Fortunately, the fire and my jump were seen by a girl who was hitchhiking on the street. She called the ambulance and also visited me every day in the hospital. We've fallen in love and plan to be married.

I am sure you'll like Agnes. She had to quit school after 10th grade to get married, but she's divorced now and has been traveling all over. It's amazing how far you can travel hitchhiking.

I've told her that I am sure the fact that she is a Hindu won't bother my loving, tolerant parents. We haven't settled on a date for the wedding yet, but I promise to call at least a week ahead of time.

Now that I've brought you up-to-date, I want to tell you that there was no dormitory fire. I did not have a skull fracture or broken leg. I was not in the hospital. I am not engaged, and there aren't even any prospects.

I am, however, getting a D in English and I'm failing Psychology, but I thought you'd like to see it all in perspective.

Your loving son,
Horace

This college person had caught the vision of keeping life in perspective. He was trying to help his parents do the same. Celebrating saints are able to do this with the power of the Holy Spirit and they see the Lord at work in their lives each day, keeping in touch with the priorities and values of life. Celebrating saints continue to look to God's Word for direction and help for priorities in their lives.

A Prayer

Lord, thanks for helping us keep our lives in perspective. It's hard sometimes not to go off on tangents. Help us, Lord, to continue to see life through Your eyes, Your death, Your resurrection. That's the only way to focus clearly on what You will have us do.

In a world of tainted models and distorted priorities it's not easy to keep the priorities of love and peace and celebration in mind. But we can do it, Lord, because we know that the power to do it is not ours; it is Your power in us. Thanks for keeping our lives in perspective. Amen.

Chapter 6

Celebrating Saints Care for People Whom God Has Seemingly Forgotten

In the early church, people would comment about certain Christians in this way, "See how they love." That is all well and good, but our task is not only to love each other but to reach out with caring hands to those unlovable and lonely people around us. When we become unlovable ourselves, we also need the care of those loving ones around us.

Celebrating saints want to share the reason for their joy by responding to the hurts and pains of others. Celebrating saints become care-takers and care-givers. They respond by words and actions to people who feel that God has forgotten them.

Reaching out to touch the lives of people can sometimes be painful. It may sometimes mean facing the scorn of "the gang" to be nice to someone who isn't a part of the gang. It might mean putting aside our own needs in order to meet the needs of others. It may even mean bearing the rejection of the very person we are trying to love.

Doing those things seems like more than we can do and often it is if we rely only on our own strength. But celebrating saints rely on God's strength. They are able to risk loving others because they know that God will provide for their needs and will enable them to bear pain. Celebrating saints are secure in God's love and can therefore reach out in love.

God works through celebrating saints in order to share His love with others. Why He chooses to do this, I don't always know. But I do know that He has empowered each of us to be His instruments of love and peace and joy. How has your life of celebration touched those who seemingly have very little to celebrate?

A Prayer

Lord, keep us celebrating, but keep us celebrating for the right reasons. Help my celebration reach out to the lonely, the hungry, the frustrated, the mixed-up people. Help me to celebrate, not only my gifts and blessings, but the fact that You allow me to share my gifts with the lonely, the hungry, and the frustrated.

Lord, help me to be an instrument of Your peace. Amen.

Chapter 7

Celebrating Saints Are People of All Ages with Different Gifts

God made people of different ages to work together, live together, play together, worship together. We need each other. Young people need adults and adults need youth. Even though we may not always feel that way, it is a fact. God brings us together around His love to help each other grow and to care for one another.

It is interesting to hear some adults talking these days. When the comment was made that there are fewer teenagers in our society right now than there have been for many years, due to the drop in number of births 13 years ago, one could sense an excitement in some adults. They hear that teenagers are dwindling in number, and they surmise that perhaps one day all teenagers will disappear. But let me assure you that this will not happen. And that is good news. If it did, adults would not be the same, children would not be the same, and young people would not be the same, because people of every age need each other.

The church is still one of the few places in our society where people of all ages can do things together. The family is still the place where there are relationships going between different age groups.

Celebrating saints need to affirm these relationships and seek new ways to put people back in touch with each other. Often grandmas and six-year-olds are out of ministry range of each other. We need to develop models and strategies and styles of living so that teenagers can play with four-year-olds and grandpas can share their experiences with young adults.

Many churches are still doing a good job of dissecting age groups. They have the men's group meeting over there, and the ladies organization meeting over here, and the youth group meeting around the corner. They meet by themselves, separated from each other, and discuss various concerns such as, "Why can't we understand other age groups?" The church needs to continue to provide opportunities for people of all ages to do things together. Why not have youth-adult Bible classes? Why not provide opportunities for youth to work with adults on various parish committees? Why not involve youth in service opportunities, along with adults, in your community?

Some churches have annual youth Sundays. And it's not that I am totally against them, but these in themselves can be dangerous. They can help to give the impression that the church again is made up of segregated age groups. Youth Sundays are fine if they provide opportunities for young people to share their gifts in leading worship. What would be even better are young people involved each week in Sunday morning worship, along with adults. Worship needs to be concerned about the needs and interests of all age groups. One way to do that is to continue to involve people of all ages in all worship opportunities.

Peer relationships are also very important for young people, as they are for adults. But perhaps we need to work harder at finding a balance between youth and adults doing things together and age groups being separated from each other. It's not an either/or question, but rather a matter of both/and.

Search the Scriptures. We don't read that the youth group was meeting out in the back under the fig tree while the adults were in ministry. God treats His people, regardless of age, as celebrating saints. We need to continue to work at providing models for youthful saints to celebrate with older saints the joy and forgiveness and love and hope that we have in Christ Jesus.

What does all this have to do with young people? How can young people make those kinds of changes in their own parish and community? Try these suggestions on for size:

1. Don't wait for adults to invite you to participate. Volunteer your services to your pastor and other church leaders.
2. Begin spending more time in your own family. Seek out opportunities to talk with older persons and younger ones. Volunteer to visit a shut-in of your parish. Ask if you may help teach a five-year-old Sunday school class or vacation Bible school. Take some neighborhood kids to the zoo.
3. Ask your parents and other adults for suggestions they have for involving young persons with people of other ages.
4. See what other churches are doing in this area of "intergenerational" ministries.
5. Continue to see and affirm the importance and power of Sunday morning worship. Here is one place where people of all ages do things together. Here they worship together, around the Word and Sacrament, Him who is the Creator and Redeemer and Sanctifier of all ages.

It is amazing how much we can learn from other age groups.

Try it out. Sit with a grandparent. Ask them about their life history. Ask them for advice. Ask them how they feel about their world today. Ask, and listen, and hear the years and years of experience flow from their lips.

Find other ways to "rub shoulders" with adults. You just might teach each other a few things. It is amazing how many stereotypes young people have of adults and adults have of young people. One way to break these down is to develop ways for youth and adults to spend more time together. Here are still more suggestions for you to consider:

1. Take your parents, or grandparents to a movie. Discuss it with them.
2. Have your church youth group sponsor "Youth-Adult Nights," where family units can gather to share and learn from each other.
3. Watch a TV show together, with your parents and other adults, and discuss it later. (You provide the popcorn.)
4. Invite parents and other adults into your high school. Have

them be your "shadow" for a day. A great learning experience for all ages!

5. Go on a trip together. This might be tough, with schedules being what they are, but give it a good try.

We continue to live in a society where "old age" is considered a disease. If that is true, we all have a terminal illness, for the one thing all of us are doing together is growing older.

Our Lord helps us to look at life, not as an illness, but as a gift. Each day is a gift from the Lord. I still remember hearing a pastor come into his office one morning and loudly proclaim, "I am proud to announce that I just shaved a 70-year-old man today!" That was his way of announcing his own birthday. That was his way of thanking God for life, each day.

A retired pastor wobbles into his doctor's office. "I'm having trouble with my left knee," the pastor remarks. After an hour of examination and $75.00 worth of treatment, the doctor calmly says to the retired pastor, "All I can say, Reverend, is that your pain is due to old age."

But the retired pastor was not ready to accept that. He glared at the doctor and eagerly said, "You're wrong, doc, because I've got a knee on the other leg that is exactly the same age as this one, and nothing is wrong with that one!"

Age is not a disease. Age is a gift. And the aging persons around us are gifts to us as well.

Many young people sense that they are similar in many ways to older persons. For example, youth and older persons are both often "forgotten." They are either too young or too old to be of much "worth" to some people. Youth and aging persons are sometimes "shelved" because of their age. Many older persons, like many young people, are lonely and are struggling for their own identity and worth in life. Many young people as well as older persons have many gifts that are not being tapped by churches and communities because of the age barriers.

As a celebrating saint, who celebrates life as a gift, see what you can do to bring age groups back together again. It will not be easy, but it will be a celebration each time it happens.

A Prayer

Lord, thanks for young people and grandparents and six-

year-olds and young adults. Even though we don't always under-
stand each other, we do know that we are bound together in Your
Word. Forgive us when we segregate ourselves from each other.
Forgive us when we don't listen to each other. Help us to see that
Your church is one body composed of members of all ages. Lord,
Your church is a festival of all saints. Help us to see each other as
caring saints with more similarities than differences. Amen.

Chapter 8

Celebrating Saints Are Not Anxious About Tomorrow

Many of you would say that this is easier said than done. I agree. Sometimes it becomes more of a problem for people to tell you not to worry than it would be if they would just leave well enough alone. But celebrating saints can be helpful to each other. As we help each other keep life in perspective, we can also help each other look at our problems and frustrations from the view of the cross.

A friend recently shared his two rules for living, guaranteed to ease your worries and anxieties.

Rule #1: Don't sweat the small stuff.

Rule #2: Everything is small stuff!

His point is obvious.

Part of the dilemma is not being able to trust the Lord at His word. A trusting relationship would mean that I can leave my worries to the Lord in prayer and devotion and know that He is actively at work in my life. But that trust sometimes breaks down.

We so easily put our trust in the wrong things. We trust our own abilities, or Lady Luck, the lottery system, and others, instead of allowing the Lord to be the one who continues to be trustworthy.

It's like the story of Anthony Clancy, an Irishman for whom the number "seven" cropped up with inordinate—almost ominous—regularity in his life. The seventh child of a seventh child, he was born on the seventh day of the week, on the seventh day of the month, in the seventh month of the year, in the seventh year of the century. On his 27th birthday he went to a race track where he discovered that the seventh horse in the seventh race was named Seventh Heaven. Its racing weight was seven stone and it odds, seven to one.

Thinking this was all too good to be true, Clancy confidently bet seven shillings on the horse.

It came in seventh.

A Prayer

Lord, help me to live out those two rules for living. Even when I add to those rules and begin even to worry about all the rules I live by, help me to realize the power of trust that You give to me.

Help me to celebrate, knowing that You are worthy to be trusted. The word of trust through our baptism has marked me forever as one of Yours. Nothing will ever take that relationship away. I can trust Your Word and Your promise that continues to assure me that I am Yours and You are mine.

Lord, help me to trust You. Help others to see Your trust through my trust. When my trust breaks down, help me to see that Your trust is always there for me. That's worth saying "Amen!"

Chapter 9

Celebrating Saints Are Also Real Sinners

There is no such thing as an "ex-sinner." We are both sinner and saint at the same time, as Martin Luther so eloquently pointed out.

But that's not always the way some people in our lives see us. Some would like celebrating saints to be only saints. They like to hear people confess their former sins as a drug addict, spouse beater, child hater, drug sniffer, sinner. Often the story is that if you're "really" a forgiven person of God, that all your sins have vanished and that you are no longer a sinner.

A friend of mine used to worry about his faith because he said he never yet had a "crisis" from which the Lord could save him and thereby assure him and others that he was saved.

Celebrating saints know that they are sinners. But celebrating saints are celebrating the fact that they are saints, forgiven by Christ through death and resurrection. We are sinners indeed, but we are forgiven sinners. That's the power of celebrating saints!

Celebrating saints no longer live by "the rules" but rather by relationships, beginning with Jesus Christ. "Living the right life," or "doing the right things," is not what makes us saints. What has made us saints is the action and fact of Jesus Christ declaring us forgiven and coming into our lives daily to empower us with His Spirit. A life as a celebrating saint is not always a life of joy and celebration, at least in the way the world defines those terms. Celebrating saints also know real pain, real problems, real crises. But celebrating saints also know real forgiveness, which continues to be their reason for celebration.

A Prayer

A sinner, Lord, that's me. No doubt about it. How anyone can deny that fact, I'll never know. But what's more important, Lord, is that I also know that I am a forgiven sinner. That's what makes me a celebrating saint. Help me share this fact with others. Help my celebration not get in the way but rather be a way for others to sense the forgiveness that is theirs in You. A sinner, yes Lord. I confess that to You. A saint, You bet, Lord, because of what You have done for us. Let's carry on with the celebration. Amen.

Chapter 10

Celebrating Saints Know That They Are Loved by God

We know that there is nothing we will ever do that will take God's love from us. That is a fact, secured for us in the death and resurrection of Jesus Christ. We also know that there is nothing we will do that will make God stop loving us more, and nothing we will do that will make God start loving us less.

His love does not depend on our actions; His love is ours because of Christ's action for us. As Major Ian Thomas used to say, "Christ's life qualified Him to die. His death has qualified us to receive the life He lived."

How do we know God loves us? Perhaps an obvious question to some, but not so obvious to many people with whom we are in contact. They do not see a loving and gracious God, but they see a God who allows suffering and death and hunger and child abuse and pain to continue, and even to grow and increase. They see a Creator who allows floods and earthquakes and auto accidents and murders to continue to happen. They read the front pages of the morning paper and again sense that even if God created the world many, many years ago He certainly is not very active in shaping it up to His standards.

As celebrating saints, youth and adults, we continue to affirm in ourselves and then to others that we are loved—in spite of how we mess things up, in spite of the front-page headlines, in spite of what others say. God is a God of love, and we know this from the Scriptures and through the power of the Holy Spirit.

Confident of God's love, we seek to show the people around us that He loves them too. They will not only know that "we are Christians by our love" but they will also know that they are loved by God through the loving action of celebrating saints around them.

A Prayer

Thanks for loving us. Even when we are unlovable, unreachable, untouchable. But You love us and Your love allows us to be lovable and reachable and touchable to other people. Continue to share Your love with us so that we can share Your love with others. Amen.

Chapter 11

Celebrating Saints See *Forgiveness* As Their Business

To me, the biggest word in the Christian dictionary is *forgiveness*. For that is our business as God's celebrating saints. We are forgiven. And that's it, period. We are forgiven as celebrating saints even when we fail to live up to the ideals mentioned in the 10 previous chapters. We are forgiven because Christ has forgiven us. This forgiveness frees us not to be so concerned about our own forgiveness but to share that forgiveness with others who are not sure of God's forgiveness.

We forgive because Christ first has forgiven us. This is the power and strength of our relationship as celebrating saints. We can go about as celebrating saints living for others because Christ lives in us. We can go around in one of two ways. First, we can go around "making a living" or else we can go around "making a difference." We are the difference because we are forgiven. To the celebrating saint, forgiveness is more than a word, it is a relationship in Jesus Christ.

Whether we are a high-school student, a homemaker, an office worker, or a sales person, we are all in the same business. That business is forgiveness. We have been qualified for this business through Jesus Christ. All education and experiences in life would not qualify us to be in the forgiveness business if it weren't for Christ. He is the sole owner and operator of the forgiveness business, and allows us to forgive other people who also are called to be celebrating saints.

We are lights to the world because of the fact that Christ is our light. "I am the light of the world," our Lord continues to remind us. Because of His light, we are able to shine out in love and forgiveness to those around us.

A little boy had a starring role in a Sunday school program. He studied his Scripture passages for weeks and was very excited about his part in the play. His mom was very excited too, but she was somewhat concerned that her son might forget his lines during the performance. Her strategy was to sit in the front row and to gesture and whisper to him any of the lines that he might forget.

The evening was at hand. The program was about to begin. The boy was ready for the big performance. And so was his mother, anxiously sitting in the front row.

The boy was doing just fine when suddenly he came to a part that he could not remember. Panic! His face reddened, he started choking up, and he couldn't remember the words. But his mother was there when he needed her, just as she had planned. She gestured and whispered softly, but to no avail. The boy could not remember. So finally in a little louder whisper she cupped her hands and said, "I am the light of the world."

"Of course," the boy thought to himself, "why couldn't I remember that?" And so, getting up his courage once again, the young man looked proudly over the audience and loudly proclaimed, "My mother is the light of the world!"

He was right! His mom was the light of the world. For all of God's celebrating saints are lights to the world as we search out and seek out those who need Christ's light of love and forgiveness. We are lights to the world, we are celebrating saints.

And I'm glad!

A Prayer

Lord, without your forgiveness we are nothing. Help us to share this forgiveness with others around us. Help us to see that forgiveness is not a *conditional* term but one that wipes away conflict and allows us to relate to others as celebrating saints.

Keep us celebrating, Lord. In the water and in the Word. Keep our celebration going in the name of Jesus. Amen.

Chapter 12

Celebrating Saints Celebrate

It was Martin Luther who said, "He who would preach the Gospel must go directly to preaching the resurrection of Christ. He who does not preach the resurrection is no apostle, for this is the chief part of our faith.... Everything depends on our retaining a firm hold on this article [of faith] in particular; for if this one totters and no longer counts, all the others will lose their value and validity" (Ewald Plass, *What Luther Says* [St. Louis: Concordia Publishing House, 1959], 3: 1215, pars. 3873–74).

Another celebrating saint, St. Paul, puts it this way, "If Christ has not been raised, then our preaching is vain and your faith is in vain. We are even found to be misrepresenting God, because we testified of God that He raised Christ, whom He did not raise if it is true that the dead are not raised.... If Christ has not been raised, your faith is futile and you are still in your sins. Then those also who have fallen asleep in Christ have perished. If for this life only we have hoped in Christ, we are of all men most to be pitied (1 Cor. 15:14–19).

Celebrating saints celebrate! They know what they are celebrating: the resurrection of Jesus Christ. Because Christ has risen, we too live in a daily resurrection.

But this is sometimes easier said than done. The joy for celebrating saints, however, is to know that the resurrection does not depend on how strongly we feel, or how close we feel towards the Lord, but rather on the fact that Christ was indeed raised from the dead. And He lives in us now!

That's the joy that celebrating saints have, and no one will ever take it away from us. Our friends, our family, our peers can forget it, and we too can sometimes try to shelve it, but the fact remains, Christ has been raised for each one of us.

This fact of the resurrection is what keeps saints celebrating. When sin, ourselves, and Satan get us down, the Spirit continues to remind us of who we are and whose we are, because of Christ's death and resurrection. Our lives take on new meaning, and we have a different perspective on things.

Celebrating saints can learn, grow, and relate to the following story. A 90-year-old woman was being placed in a nursing home by her family. She was looking forward to it, as she looked forward to every day as a gift of life from the Lord. As they helped her into the home her eyes continued to twinkle and look out over her new environment. She quickly spotted a 95-year-old man sitting by himself in the cafeteria.

As she slowly but enthusiastically made her way over to the man's table, her eyes continued to twinkle. She looked at him with her celebrative eyes and she said, "You remind me a lot of my third husband."

The man, not sure what to make of this intrusion into his life, sat there a moment and stared back. Then, he finally got up enough nerve to ask, "How many husbands have you had?"

With a gleam in her eye, the old woman happily exclaimed, "Two!"

Celebrating saints celebrate! They celebrate, not because they have forgotten about death and sin in the world, but because they have remembered and know the power of the resurrection of Jesus Christ. Celebrating saints are called to spread the celebration to others. We proclaim loudly and clearly, and even softly and intimately, the truth of the fact that Jesus Christ loves and forgives each of us. We reach out to those who are not celebrating, because of the pain and problems in their own lives. We reach out with our own hands and lives to sense their pain and to cry with them in order to enable them to see the source of power that the Lord can give them also.

Let's continue the celebration. Christ lives, we live. What more could we ask?

A Prayer

Lord, help us to see that celebrations are more than loud noises and balloons. Help us to see that celebrations for Your people begin with the relationship we have with Jesus Christ.

Lord, as these pages have shared some of the joy and power of the resurrection, allow us to share the same joy and power through our daily lives.

Help us to proclaim with the writer of Ecclesiastes that there is a time for birth and a time for death. A time for sorrow and a time for joy. A time for mourning and a time for dancing. Help us to see that You provide so many opportunities for us to share our faith with others and to help others to see that life is a celebration.

Thanks, Lord, for Your power, Your presence, Your promise. Thanks Lord for selecting us to be celebrating saints. In the name of Jesus we continue our celebration! Amen.

Part 2

Chapter 1

Celebrating Saints Ask Tough Questions

The following is a list of questions that young people have raised over the past two years at various youth gatherings. They are shared here, not so much for answers, but rather to show others questions that saints of God continue to ask. These are real questions raised by real young people with real situations.

How do you respond to these questions? You may want to discuss them with family and friends.

This also points out that celebrating saints do not have all the answers. As we celebrate together, we can be bold enough to raise these questions and concerns. We can be daring enough to reach out and seek answers and directions for these concerns. We can be courageous enough to confess that at times we doubt and wonder about life and our daily existence.

As you look through these questions, think of ways you would respond. Think of what you would say to persons raising these questions around you. Ask other celebrating saints for their input and help in dealing with these questions.

You may even want to add a few of your own questions at the end of this list.

1. Why does God allow young people to die?
2. Why doesn't God say Yes to all my prayers?
3. What should I do with my life?
4. How can I deal with my parents divorce?
5. Will I find the right person to marry—and will it last? (How do I deal with sex in the meantime?)
6. What's wrong with homosexuality?
7. Why can't I live my life the way I want to?
8. How can I get others to like me more?
9. Why should I plan on what I want to be as an adult, since the world will be in a mess anyway?
10. What about premarital sex and the Gospel?
11. Where can I turn for help in dating pressures?
12. Why doesn't anyone listen to me anymore?
13. What can I do to help prevent nuclear war and to protect my loved ones?
14. How do I know what God wants from my life and what I'm supposed to be? How can I "hear" God?
15. How can I improve my relationship with my parents? How do I know they are really saved?
16. My friends have different values than I do. How can I change them? Why can't I keep them as friends?
17. Why can't we be more informal with our worship services?
18. Why is the pastor's sermon always so long?
19. What can I do with my parents?
20. How can I help my friends who start to smoke and drink?
21. Why can't we have Bible studies in our public schools?
22. Why don't other churches want us to come? (A Black and White issue.)
23. Why is the KKK so strong, and how come they can recruit in school?
24. Whatever happened to news about the good students?
25. Why do I have to hurt when my parents fight?
26. I don't want to be torn between Mom and Dad and going to two homes. Don't I have any rights?
27. Why do people assume that if you are Black they'd better watch you? ... You're trouble.
28. Is our world going to be blown up?

29. Why do I have to go to confirmation class? What good will it do me?
30. Why don't the adults do things with us?
31. What can I do in my church? They won't let me do anything.
32. Why do my parents always have to hassle me about my grades in school?
33. Why can't young people vote in their churches?
34. What's the end of the world going to be like?
35. How can I get a stronger faith?
36. How do I know what God wants me to be?
37. How do I know what God wants me to do?
38. Do you have to be poor to be a Christian?
39. Why did God let my father die?
40. Why do we pay to support the church but we can't vote on how to spend the money?
41. How can I share my faith more openly?
42. Why do adults take themselves so seriously?
43. How can I get to know my pastor better?
44. Why do a lot of adults think kids are always getting into trouble?
45. How can I better understand the Scriptures?

Now think of some of your own questions that you may want to add to this list and use this list as a discussion point with family and friends.

Celebrating saints do ask tough questions. Celebrating saints don't have all the answers, but we have the source of understanding the presence and power in our lives through Jesus Christ, as we struggle with some of these hard questions of life.

Additional Questions to Consider

1. How can I communicate with God more easily in prayer?
2. How can I come to know God better?
3. How do we get the "elders" of the church to appreciate youth and our future?
4. When I am sick, is that a punishment from God for sinning?
5. What is the difference between Lutheran, Catholic, and other denominations?
6. I don't understand that God, Son, and Spirit are one. Please explain.
7. If God loves me, why can't I get my locker open?
8. How do I fit into my church?

9. How can I better prepare myself to spread the Word of God to friends?
10. How can we get more people involved in youth groups?
11. How can I tell what God wants me to do with my life?
12. Why do we repeat the same old Bible studies? They all seem to be alike.
13. Why don't they have youth gatherings more often?
14. How can we get more people involved?
15. How come our parents don't understand us?
16. How come we sometimes don't understand our parents?
17. If there really is a God how come He is letting bad situations happen to me and my family?
18. Is life really worth living?
19. Why aren't adults willing to work with today's youth?
20. How is God real in my life?
21. If God loves us and all that stuff, why are there wars? Why does God let bad things happen?
22. How can I grow closer to God, and get to know Him better?
23. Why does God make us go through so much pain—death, parents' divorce—if He loves us so much?
24. Why did a certain person have to die or become ill?
25. How can I fit into God's plan? How can I be of any help as a young person?

As you can see, most of these questions deal with relationships, identity, and some of the struggles in life. Perhaps you have asked or heard about most of them yourself.

How do you respond to them? Where do you go for help in answering these questions yourself?

As you deal and struggle with many of these questions, young people need to continue to see that the Lord has put adults in their lives to help them through these issues. Adults are not there just to give "answers," but rather to listen, to share their faith, and hopefully to direct young people in positive channels to deal with these concerns.

The Scriptures do hold the answers to these questions. In one or another, *the* answer is Jesus Christ. Often, however, the problem is how to allow Jesus Christ to be real to people so that they see Him as *the* answer. He is the source of all comfort, hope, and strength. Answers do not come quickly or easily, but we continue to see Christ as the power and guidance in our lives.

Seek out the help of professional church workers as well as other caring and genuine adults to help you through these questions. Take time to pray to the Lord for guidance and direction. Do not wait for adults to give you the answers; instead, go after them yourself by asking and raising these issues with them. Don't be afraid to question. Take your concerns to the Lord and also to the people that the Lord puts around you for support, comfort, and relationships.

Celebrating saints are able to ask these kinds of questions because they know that the Lord is present to deal with these and all questions in life. The answers do not come easily. The directions in life are often muddied and hazy. But celebrating saints continue to seek the power and comfort and direction of the Lord.

The celebrating saint's life is not one big happy "rose garden." Celebrating saints are called to a life of pain, of frustration, of fears, of struggles. It is only through the power of the Holy Spirit that we are able to deal with these struggles and continue to celebrate the fact that we know who we are, as well as whose we are!

Yes, continue to "celebrate" as you yourself struggle along with others over the many questions in life.

A poster I saw recently says it well:

"Fear knocked on the door

Christ answered—no one was there!"

Worksheet for Discussion of Questions

Here is your chance to write down some of your own questions, or to jot down some of your thoughts that surface after reading the previous list of questions. Share your thoughts with someone. Seek to help each other grapple with these and other questions you have.

1. Which of the questions captures some of your main concerns in life?

2. Which other questions would you add?

3. Which ones would you subtract? (Those that have been answered for you.)

4. Which ones are being asked the most by people you know? How can you best respond to them?

5. Further thoughts you want to remember to share with someone.

Chapter 2

Prayers for Celebrating Saints Today

Here are some prayers for every celebration, and then some. As you share them may they help you in your faith, in your relationships with your Lord and those around you, and in your knowing that you continue to be a "celebrating" saint in the Lord Jesus.

Celebrate Life!

Lord, thanks for this new day.
Help me to see it as a gift from You;
help me to share it with those around me;
help me to enjoy it as I see You in my life;
help me to give it away to someone today;
help me to celebrate life every day! Amen.

How Do You Spell C-E-L-E-B-R-A-T-E?

Lord, the word "celebrate" brings other words to mind for me. The only way "celebrate" is spelled correctly is to affirm that it begins with a "C," which stands for Christ. With You as the starting point, all celebrations will be real celebrations.

While we're spelling, let's add a few other words to the letters:

C— is for Christ, the beginning of our celebrations;
E— is for Easter, the reason for our joy;
L— is for Listen, to You and to each other;
E— is for Everywhere, which reminds us of Your presence;
B— is for Burdens, which are kept in perspective through You;
R— is for Rejoice, a great way to share our faith;
A— is for Affirm, which You do to us through Your love;
T— is for Trust, which comes from above;
E— is for Exciting, which is the way all celebrations in You end.

Help us to begin our celebrations always with You. Amen.

When I Don't Feel Like a Saint

Lord, there are days when I don't feel so "saintly." There are certainly days when I don't look or act so saintly either.

Help me to realize that my faith or my "saintliness" do not depend on me; rather, they depend on the fact that You love me and have died and risen for me. This takes the pressure off. This allows me to know that my faith does not depend on how I feel, or on how I look, or even on how I act. (And that's a good thing!)

Thanks, Lord, for calling me a "saint" even when I don't feel like one. Amen.

What Will I Do with My Life?

Lord, it's tough to know what You want me to do with my life. You've given me gifts to use, but how am I supposed to know how to use them? Couldn't You have sent along an instruction sheet to tell me how to put them in practice?

Lord, I see a lot of people going around trying to make a living, and that's okay, I guess. But I've got the feeling that You would rather have me going around trying to make a difference. Help me, Lord, to use my gifts to make a difference in the lives of others. Amen.

A Prayer for a Rainy Day

Lord, this day is a washout. I had so much to do outside, and now it continues to pour. Another day down the drain. But while I am complaining, Lord, help to see the good side of rainy days.

With You, there always is a good side of life's experiences. Help me to thank You for the rain today, on behalf of farmers, plants, construction workers who needed a day off, worms who need some air and moisture, all of my mom's pretty plants, and for the maker of boots and umbrellas.

It's a good day to listen to the rain, to read, to visit, and to thank You for water. But, Lord, please don't overdo it now. Give the weatherman something to smile about tomorrow. Amen.

On Taking a Trip

I know someone who is leaving for Australia soon, Lord. Be with her as she travels. I know others who will be leaving for college again soon. Grant them a strong measure of Your peace.

I know someone who is moving to the West Coast. Guard and protect them on their way.

I know someone who moved into a new home recently. Bring him love and joy to warm the new house.

Lord, it is important that I know these people. Thanks for providing their friendship to me. But it's even more important that You know these people—and that You died and rose for them all, so that wherever they may go, You continue to know and love them.

Help them to know this too, Lord! Amen.

A Prayer on the Day the Report Card Comes

Lord, perhaps this prayer is a little late. Perhaps it should have gotten to You before I took the tests. But, anyway, I do want to thank You for giving me the chance to learn and to study and grow in my knowledge, even though I don't always see it as a "blessing."

When I open my report card, I am not asking You for straight A's. I am asking You to give me an accepting heart, to give me parents with a forgiving heart, to give me friends with a humble heart, and to keep pushing me to use my brains a little more actively during the next grading period. Amen.

When "Celebration" Is Spelled "Sell-Abration"

Lord, sometimes I think that store advertisements overdo it.

After all, do we always need all of the items that they say we do? Do I really need a new tennis racket or a new sweater? Are my motives based on special "sales" rather than on my own needs?

Don't let the stores have all the sell-abrations. Sure, let them enjoy their jobs and let the managers make a decent living, but in the meantime, help me to see that my celebrations do not depend on my possessions and things I can buy, but rather that they depend on Your promises contained in your Word. I'm glad that Your kind of celebrations are "free" for us. Amen.

On Celebrating a Special Birthday

All birthdays are special, Lord, because life is a gift from You.

Give all people celebrating a birthday today a real special day of love and joy. Let them see You in the gifts they receive and in the food that they eat. Let them see You as the "light" to the world as they blow out their candles, help them to see You wrapped up in their lives, as their gifts become unwrapped.

Don't let Hallmark cards get all the credit. Keep showing us, Lord, that You are the source of all celebrations, including birthdays! Amen.

Who Says I Have to Smile?

Lord, are there many people who are always smiling? When I see one, I get angry and upset. No one should smile and laugh all the time. Not that they shouldn't be rejoicing in Your presence. But life just isn't cut that way. Can I help it if my mouth sags and my face droops when I see all the pain and sin and problems around me?

Tell me it is okay not to smile sometimes, Lord. Tell me that You still love and forgive me even if I don't look like it. Because Your love for me is more than skin-deep. It reaches throughout all of my life.

That doesn't give me an excuse for not smiling, Lord. It just helps me to realize that to celebrate our faith is much more than a smile and a chuckle. It's real and deep, it's mine because of Your death and resurrection.

No one is going to take that away from me—smile or no smile. Amen.

On Wings Like an Eagle

I like to watch eagles, Lord. They are so graceful and free.

I like to read Isaiah 40:28–31. It is so graceful and free also.

You remind us through Your Word that You are the one who continues to lift us up when we become weak and weary and ready to fold.

Thanks, Lord, for eagles. Keep them flying and free. And thanks, Lord, for giving us the power to regain our strength from our weariness, for giving us a wind and a prayer as we fly through another day with You. Amen.

On Graduation Day

Talk about something to celebrate, Lord, it's graduation day!

Hooray for my teachers and friends and principal and school activities, but a bigger hooray for the fact that it is over! I'm finished. I've graduated! I really do know, Lord, that it really isn't over. But it still feels good to think that way, at least right now.

I know that I will miss many things about school. I know that I'll keep remembering the "good old" days, just like my parents.

With Your help, I know that I'll also continue to see You in my life as you lead me into new directions and goals and relationships with others. Hooray, Lord, not only for graduations, but, more importantly, hooray for You, because you continue to be with me one graduation at a time and one day at a time. Amen.

On Celebrating Death

Lord, the title of this prayer may offend some people. But it is true. Death can be celebrated. I know. I just saw it happen.

She died during the Lenten season, but her funeral was a joyous celebration of Easter. It was complete with lilies, banners, and trumpets. It was joy-filled. It was tear-filled. It was a celebration of life, in the midst of death.

The pain of death is turned into the joy of celebration, Lord, through You.

That is not to say that we no longer suffer and cry and hurt, but it is to say that You allow us to see that death is part of our life in

You. Because of Your death and resurrection, we can truly celebrate our death and look forward to our resurrection.

Help me to celebrate death, Lord. It's not always easy. Help me to reach out to those who cannot understand why we had an Easter celebration for a saint who had just died.

Thanks, Lord for allowing us to celebrate both life and death. Amen.

The Little Things in Life

Lord, it's easy to celebrate big things in life, such as birthdays, anniversaries, trips, special gifts. What I need more help on is being able to celebrate some of the little "niceties" You continue to give me, like

> being able to buy a new pair of shoes;
> finishing an assignment at school, on time;
> a friendly "good morning" from my Mom;
> a smile from a friend;
> a listening ear when I need to talk;
> a nice-sounding album;
> the smell of the fresh air after a rain.

I could go on and on. Come to think of it, Lord, these "little" things really become "big" things in my life to celebrate, for without them, I'm not sure I could make it.

Thanks, Lord, for the little things, and the big things, in life. They all are big blessings from You. Amen.

On Mowing the Lawn

Lord, maybe the "grass is always greener on the other side," but why is the grass always longer on my side? It's grass-cutting time again, and even though it gives me a chance to exercise and get outside, it also becomes a bore. Even if I get paid to do it, it's not that much fun. Why do You allow the grass to grow anyway? Couldn't You just put it on hold for a while? But keep me mowing, Lord, it at least does give me time to think and dream and wonder if Astroturf might just be the best invention You gave to us in a long time. Amen.

It's All in the Way We Look at It

Someone once said that creativity was "looking at one thing and seeing something else."

I think that is a good definition of the Christian life also, Lord. For You allow us to be able to look at things through the cross and the empty tomb. That turns our pain into acceptance, our sorrow into joy, our hurts into caring actions.

Help me, Lord, to see life from Your eyes. Help me to see people the way You see all of us—not as condemned sinners, but as forgiven saints. It all depends on how we look at things. Right, Lord? Amen.

Special License Plates

I'm not sure what state started it, Lord, but have You noticed all of the personal plates around these days? Just during the past few days, I've seen plates that read:

Hey You

Mine

Zoom

Paid 4

Back Off

Slodown

Ez Cum

Rev

No 1

What would Your license plate say, Lord? How do You want us to define and name You? Would they be words like "forgiven," "servant," "care," "love," "peace"? Maybe even one that would say, to everyone driving cars around these days: U R MINE!

Thanks for keeping us mindful of Your love through cars and people and signs and even license plates, that You truly are our Lord. Amen.

Sunday Morning Celebration

Lord, Sunday morning should be the best celebration of the week. Sometimes it is, but other times it isn't. How can I help to make Sunday morning a festive experience for me?

Even though it is easy to put the blame on other things, like long sermons or drawn-out music or hard pews or the "same old thing," help me to realize that a lot of the "un-celebration" part of worship has to do with me.

It is probably correct to say that you get out of something what you put into it. And sometimes I really do not invest much on Sunday morning. I'm too tired, I've got other things on my mind; and all this gets in the way.

One way to help me get more out of Sunday would be if I would be asked to become more involved. Maybe I need to participate more. Maybe I need to see that any kind of "liturgy" is to help me worship You, rather than getting in the way of worshiping You.

Help me, Lord, to have the courage to share my feelings with my pastor and others around me. Then, as we work together on this concern, perhaps we can all help each other see that every Sunday morning is a real celebration, because You are there with us, in the Word and in the sacraments, to build us up, to pick us up, to move us out, even when we don't feel like celebrating. Amen.

Christian Music

I'm constantly surrounded by music, Lord. Some of it is great, and other albums are just plain obscene and frightening. Help me struggle, Lord, with the gift of music. What makes music "Christian," anyway? Is it just the words, or the motives, or the persons, or how it is heard and used? I'm confused, Lord. There are groups who call themselves "Christian" groups, and that's fine, but does that make all of the other groups "non-Christian"?

Someone once told me there is no such thing as "Christian" music. The only thing Christian is that which can be baptized—in other words, people. I want to see music as a gift created by You. I want to enjoy it. I also want to be able to choose between what music has solid, positive Christ-like content, which I can accept, and which music is simply trash.

Help me to celebrate the gift of music and help me to celebrate with music. But also guide me into knowing which is which and how best I can respond to everything that is bombarding me through records and videos.

Help me see music as still a gift, even though many are misusing that gift.

Help me to continue to "sing a new song to the Lord." Amen.

Celebration Made Easy

Sure, Lord, people say it's easy to celebrate and feel good when everything is going well. But what about the times when the world is falling apart, when you agree with the poster that suggest, "In case of an accident, I'm not surprised!"

You give us the power to celebrate continually, each day, only in different styles. Help us to realize that if we think celebrations are only for the "good" days, that we really do not understand what Your kind of celebrations are all about.

Your kind of celebrations grow out of Your death and resurrection. And from Your presence in our lives: that's where our reason for celebrating comes from.

We celebrate, with loud shouts or quiet tears, because You are our God and You have made us Your people. That's something to celebrate on good days and on bad ones. Amen.

Life Is for Giving

Life is for giving, Lord. And the life You give us is forgiving.

Forgiveness is the key to our relationship with You and with one another. Were it not for forgiveness, there would be no way that we could celebrate. Our sins would continue to destroy us and condemn us constantly.

But the life we have in You is a forgiven life; we are able to give our lives for others because You have given Your life for us.

It's a great word, Lord. Better yet, it's a great relationship which You have developed between us.

Keep us forgiving, Lord. Keep our lives for giving for others, too. Amen.

Youth Is Not a Disease

Lord, from the way society talks about young people one would think that teenagers are a disease. Check the paper and news commentaries. We continually hear about the young people who have messed up, who have gone astray, and we want to reach out to them. But that's not the full picture, Lord.

Help adults who are around young people see them, not as problems, but as people. Help adults see young people as redeemed, forgiven people of God, just like all the other age groups.

Not because we deserve it, but because You have earned it for us. Help adults see youth the way You see all of us.

While you're at it, Lord, help young people to see adults in exactly the same way. Amen.

Easier or Easter?

Lord, how similar these two words are! You must have planned it that way. When things get rough, we can easily murmur, "Lord, make life a little easier for us, please?" And You respond to us with Your love and forgiveness. You cross out the "I" at the center of our world and replace it with the "T" of Your cross.

You give us an Easter life, instead of a easier one.

Thanks for the resurrection, Lord.

Thanks for calling us, not to an easier life, but to an Easter life. Amen.

We Are the People of God

What a great statements of who we are and whose we are! You have called all people as Your people. You say it so well in Colossians 3:12–17, when You state, "[You are] God's chosen ones, holy and beloved . . ."

That statement of fact is enough to get me through this day, Lord. I'm going to make it, because of what You have done for me.

Your owning of me frees me to live now for others around me—to reach out, to celebrate, to risk loving others.

I am a person of God. We are the people of God. What a great sound. What a great fact. Help me to celebrate that fact today. Amen.

Putting Young People in Their Place

That's right Lord. Youth and adults need help in putting
 young people "in their place."

But instead of seeing this as a negative statement, we see it as a positive and affirming phrase. Because "the place" of young people is in the mainstream of life, through their families, congregations, schools, and communities.

Help all of us, Lord, youth and adults, to put young people in their place—beginning at the foot of the cross, going up to the empty tomb, and then out into the ministry of life. Amen.

Family Ties

Lord, we sing, "Blest Be the Tie That Binds," but sometimes the binding becomes a rope or an apron string that needs to be cut. This prayer is shared to affirm the binding You do through our families. Thank You for that.

Also help family members continue to be bound together, not by lots of rules and regulations but more by Your love and forgiveness. As parents begin to loosen the strings and ropes from their kids, help them all to be joined together by the love that comes from You.

Help our family ties that come from You to be the source of strength as we deal with family sighs and family cries and family tries.

Thanks for keeping us together and close to each other as we see our motto as, "One for the other, all for Christ." Amen.

TV or Not TV

Lord, did You create television to be a blessing or a curse for us? I suppose it just depends on how we use it.

It's a blessing if we see it as a marvel of your creation, that allows us to be entertained and informed and aware of people from all over the globe.

It can be a curse, though, if we see it for selfish pleasures, R-rated movies, unrealistic "soaps" and as an escape from our everyday responsibilities. We know, Lord, that kids and young people and adults spend much more time in front of the tube than they (or should I say "we"?) spend in worship, in devotion, in serving and caring for others. Something's wrong somewhere, Lord, with our priorities.

Help me, Lord, to see TV as a gift from You. Help me to assess how I use my time, both when it comes to TV as well as other times. Help me to help others to be selective in how I use the gifts that You freely give us. Your favorite prayer really hits home to me, Lord, ". . . lead me not into temptation." No commercial, Lord, to end this prayer, just a loud Amen!

Praise the Lord!

What a phrase, Lord: "Praise the Lord!" It says it all. It says it well. But sometimes it is said too often and in too many shallow ways. Forgive my judging words, but at times I am not ready to shout and jump up and say, "Praise the Lord!" Sometimes I feel like the psalmist who is angry and hurt and struggling with existence itself. And then to be told that, in order really to have faith, we need to shout, "Praise the Lord!" is not at all helpful.

Help me and others to see that our whole lives are ones of praise to You. And that You love and forgive us, regardless of whether or not we are singing or shouting our faith to others. Help me and others realize that sometimes the best way to praise You is simply to be quiet and listen to Your soft words of comfort and hope and joy and peace. To that I whisper, "Praise the Lord."

Maybe tomorrow I'll feel like shouting, and if so, I will, but for now, Lord, I think You understand. Thanks for listening. Amen.

Cope with Hope

Lord, it is hard to cope with all of the problems and pressures around us. Grades, clothes, future plans, parents, friends—they all can add to our frustrations. Help me to cope with big and small things in my life, Lord.

Help me to cope by hanging on to the hope that You give to me. I don't mean hope as in "wish," but rather as in the fact that I can hope in You because You have died and risen for me.

Help me to cope, Lord, first by seeing You in all of my life, and then by trusting in the hope that is in me—because of You! Amen.

Gifted to Give

You have given us so many gifts Lord, and for these we are

thankful. At times we may wish that we would have more gifts, or different gifts, or sometimes we may even feel jealous that You gave others gifts that we would like to have. But we really do thank You for providing us the talents to share with others.

Help me to see, Lord, that gifts aren't any good unless we use them. Help me to use the gifts that are mine, from You. Help me to be thankful for the gifts that I do have, rather than be envious of the gifts I do not have.

We are gifted to give, Lord. You have given us so many blessings. Help us now to be a blessing to others. Amen.

Parents are People, Too!

I know that parents are people, Lord. I know they mean well and that they love their kids. But why is it sometimes difficult to understand them? Why is it that sometimes their love comes out as anger, resentment, or disappointment?

Maybe they just try too hard to love us? Or maybe they still see us through their own eyes when they were younger? Whatever it is, Lord, we sure need a big dose of understanding and acceptance.

Help me to show my parents that I really do love them, even if it always doesn't come out that way. Help me to say what needs to be said but also what doesn't need to be said. While You're at it, throw in a big dose of forgiveness too! Amen.

Me? A Celebrating Saint?

At times, Lord, I just don't feel like celebrating. I sure don't feel like a saint, either.

No wonder it's tough for me sometimes to get involved in worship on Sunday morning. I just don't feel like the person whom God has forgiven and redeemed.

When these times hit me, Lord, help me to cling to the fact that my faith in You does not depend on how I feel, or on how I look or even act. Help me to know that my faith depends on what You have done for me by dying and rising. Then I will know that I really am a saint, and a celebrating one at that, even when I don't feel like it or look like it or act like it.

Thanks, Lord, for calling me a saint, and for allowing me to celebrate my life with You. Thanks for accepting me even when I don't feel very acceptable. Help me to put all of my celebrations in Your hands. Amen.

Creating Celebrative Prayers on Your Own

Now it is your turn. Use these pages to write out some of your prayers and prayer thoughts. No need to be formal or long. Just jot down thoughts that come to you throughout the coming days.

Share some of these thoughts with others. It can be most helpful to share your concerns, questions, as well as joys with those around you.

1. A prayer for the morning:

2. A prayer for the night:

3. General prayers:

4. Specific prayers:

5. Anything goes: